THE "MYSTERY MAN"
BEHIND BITCOIN

CRYPTOMANIA

AN ESSENTIAL
GUIDE TO CRYPTOCURRENCY

I0396739

ADHIRAJ PAL

INDIA · SINGAPORE · MALAYSIA

Notion Press

No.8, 3rd Cross Street,
CIT Colony, Mylapore,
Chennai, Tamil Nadu – 600004

First Published by Notion Press 2021
Copyright © Adhiraj Pal 2021
All Rights Reserved.

ISBN 978-1-63832-597-0

This book has been published with all efforts taken to make the material error-free after the consent of the author. However, the author and the publisher do not assume and hereby disclaim any liability to any party for any loss, damage, or disruption caused by errors or omissions, whether such errors or omissions result from negligence, accident, or any other cause.

While every effort has been made to avoid any mistake or omission, this publication is being sold on the condition and understanding that neither the author nor the publishers or printers would be liable in any manner to any person by reason of any mistake or omission in this publication or for any action taken or omitted to be taken or advice rendered or accepted on the basis of this work. For any defect in printing or binding the publishers will be liable only to replace the defective copy by another copy of this work then available.

Contents

1. Slangs Used in Cryptocurrency Market	5
2. Concept of Money	7
3. Legality	10
4. Short Guide to Start an ICO	27
5. Ethereum	40
6. Ripple (XRP)	44
7. Litecoin	48
8. Dogecoin	50
9. Tron	52
10. Bittorrent	55
11. Cardano (ADA)	57
12. Matic Network	60
13. Opinions of the Global Personalities on Blockchain and Cryptocurrency	63

SLANGS USED IN CRYPTOCURRENCY MARKET

1. HODL – Hold On for Dear Life
2. Altcoin – Every other coin other than BITCOIN.
3. FOMO – Fear Of Missing Out.
4. JOMO – Joy of Missing Out
5. Moon – Everyone wants their coin price to go up in the outer space.
6. Bag Holder – Someone who is holding a lot of coins, in the hope that it will go up in the future.
7. Shitcoin – A worthless or dead coin with no real value
8. Dumping – Downward price movement or a decision to sell a coin.
9. DYOR – Do Your Own Research

10. FUD – Fear, uncertainty and doubt.
11. Whale – A super wealthy trader with a lot of money to spend.
12. Mining – Verifying transactions on a blockchain, resulting in rewards, for those who lend their computing power.
13. Long – A decision to hold onto a coin.
14. REKT – When a coin goes down sharply and you have a bad loss.
15. Lambo – The car many people want to buy when they strike it rich.
16. Swing – When the price of a coin is moving up and down at a rapid rate.
17. Pumping – A coordinated effort to boost a coin by buying a lot of it all at once.
18. Bearish – When the sentiment of a coin is negative.
19. Bullish – When the sentiment of a coin is positive.
20. Exchange – Websites that allow you to purchase and sell crypto currencies.
21. IFAT – Any currency that is issued by a government
22. TA – Technical Analysis
23. ATH – All Time High
24. FA – Fundamental Analysis

CONCEPT OF MONEY

Money is a medium of exchange in the form of coins and bank notes, which are used to buy goods and services of different kinds. Money, essentially is a store of value which gained the value once we as a society collectively agreed for its use to purchase the goods and services of the entire world. Money is an economic unit which facilitates all the financial functions of the world. The US dollar became the most powerful currency because people of the world agreed upon the fact that they want to hold the US dollar as it is the safest and most stable currency of the world. It is only because of the belief and the mutual agreement of the people that the US dollar became the most powerful and the most widely used currency. Now with all the technological advancements which we are witnessing day by day, the block chain technology has helped in introducing a new, decentralized mode of digital money or currency called the *Cryptocurrency* which the people have started accepting as a 'token of value'.

What is a Cryptocurrency?

A **Cryptocurrency** is a digital asset which is designed to work as a mode of exchange where individual coin ownership records are stored in a ledger which is present in a form of computerized databases, using strong cryptography to secure transaction records, to control the creation of additional coins, and to verify the transfer of coin ownership. *Cryptography* is associated with a process of converting ordinary plain text into unintelligible text and vice-versa, in this method data is stored and transferred in particular form so that only those, for whom the data is intended can read and process it.

Cryptocurrency does not exist in a physical form (like fiat currency or paper money) and is not issued by any Central authority. Cryptocurrencies use decentralised control. When a cryptocurrency is mined or created prior to issuance or is issued by a single issuer, it is generally considered to be Centralized. When implemented with decentralized control, each cryptocurrency works through a distributed ledger technology, typically a *Blockchain* which serves as a public financial transaction database, which holds the record of each and every transaction that has taken place. Cryptocurrency in millennial language is considered as 'Digital Cash' where no one else, other than the parties, needs to be involved to complete the transaction. The blockchain works as one big excel sheet which everyone can see, once a record has been put up there it can never be changed. In simpler terms if A sends some Cryptocurrency for instance a Bitcoin, to B, then the Blockchain would publicly declare that A has sent X amount to B, therefore there are no intermediaries required for the completion of this process. It is one of the most traceable data records to have ever been there, therefore these misconceptions that one can make money disappear through crypto are not true at all.

The king of all the crypto currencies is considered to be the BITCOIN, rest all other currencies are referred to as Altcoins. All these Altcoins inherited the title of crypto currency from the Bitcoin, while on the other hand it should have been termed as crypto 'tokens'.

LEGALITY

The battle for legalisation of cryptocurrencies is going on ever since the success stories of Bitcoin had started surfacing all over the internet. The problem that we face with crypto currencies is that they do not have a regulatory system, as they are not made for the purpose of regulation. Therefore, it is difficult for the governments or the countries to legalise and make these currencies as their Legal Tender of Money.

Some countries who have made the cryptocurrencies legal include *Japan*, which is one of the fastest developing technology markets in the world. The country's government has set up a specific PSA (Payment Services Act) based framework which allows some cryptocurrencies and a number of exchanges to be used for payment and trading purposes. Japan is now widely considered as a hub for cryptocurrency trading/exchange in Asia.

The *United States of America (USA)*, in 2013, had accepted Bitcoin as a decentralized virtual currency that can be used for performing transactions. It was classified as a commodity by CFTC (Commodity Futures Trading Commission) in September, 2015.

Bitcoin is also taxable as a property in the US. In simple terms, Bitcoin is legal in the USA, however, there is no clarification about the legalization of other cryptocurrencies.

Germany is one of the few European countries that not only allow cryptocurrencies but are also actively involved in the development of blockchain solutions for a better future. Germany has completely legalized bitcoin allowing citizens to transact and trade using this coin. The recognition of Bitcoin by the German government has also improved the value of these coins in the worldwide market.

France had issued a regulation note on 11 July 2014, in which the country has legalized the operation of virtual currencies such as Bitcoin, along with cryptocurrency exchanges, taxation and provided authority to those who are involved in the trading and use of such crypto currencies.

Malta has added its name to the long list of countries that are finally accepting Bitcoin and other cryptocurrencies as a legal mode for digital transactions. The cabinet of Malta recently approved the bills regarding the regulation of cryptocurrency and ICOs (Initial Coin Offerings) in the country, which officially makes it a fully-fledged crypto-legal country.

Canada in August 2017, accepted Impak Coin as its first legalized cryptocurrency. The Quebec regulation authority had previously legalized Bitcoin for some limited business models including ATMs and exchanges. However, the Bank of Montreal and some other Canadian states do not allow their customers to use their bank cards for performing cryptocurrency transactions.

Belarus, as per a recent order by the government will legalise the use of cryptocurrencies with effect from March 28, 2019. In addition to the leading crypto-coins, many exchanges, ICOs, and smart contracts will also be legal in the country. The step was taken with the aim to enforce the development of a digital economy. They are also considering to make crypto activities completely tax-free.

Holland, is also one of the countries which has shown a positive attitude towards Bitcoin and other virtual currencies. There is a special region, called "Bitcoin City" in Holland where all the Bitcoin transactions including retail purchases, trading and business are completely legal.

However, the Holland government has not yet regulated or officially legalized the use of any cryptocurrency.

Vietnam has legalised the trading and purchase of cryptocurrencies, however, the government of Vietnam doesn't allow its citizens to use any virtual currency yet, as a payment tool or as a legal tender for money. This means creating new cryptocurrencies and launching ICOs in Vietnam is completely legal and so is the trading of cryptocurrency at popular exchanges. The government is also reportedly working on legalizing Bitcoin as a method of payment by 2019 end.

Singapore has legalised the use and trading of Bitcoin and other popular virtual currencies, but the government doesn't control the operations or price of these currencies. Cryptocurrencies, by nature, are supposed to be unregulated. Therefore, it shouldn't be a problem for merchants and consumers in Singapore to freely use cryptocurrencies. The use of Bitcoin in Singapore is taxable in some cases.

The bank of *Thailand* had legalized the use of Bitcoin in the country in 2017. The exchange and trading of digital currencies are allowed provided that proper care is taken no one indulges in fraudulent activities. Only licensed bitcoin exchanges in Thailand are allowed to exchange cryptocurrencies for Thai Baht. However, the central bank of Thailand doesn't allow its users and associated financial institutions to participate in any kind of cryptocurrency-related business.

India after the circular in, 2018, had finally decided to go along with the cryptocurrency and first on the list would be the bitcoin. The country is working on making some special provisions to keep up the trend and is recently planning to levy a tax on virtual currency trading. The Indian government may sooner or later regularize the Cryptocurrency in the country with some special provisions, laws & regulations.

Russia made an announcement in November 2016, in which the Federal Tax Service of Russia declared bitcoins as "not illegal". Even though it doesn't say that bitcoins or any other Cryptocurrency are Legal & Illegal in the country, people are allowed to purchase, sale or trade in virtual currencies at their own risk. The government doesn't regulate, support or control the exchange of cryptocurrencies but these are not prohibited from operating. Some other countries where BTC is considered legal are:

- Gibraltar
- Ukraine
- Switzerland
- The Netherlands
- Lithuania
- Estonia
- The United Kingdom
- Bermuda
- Slovenia
- Singapore
- Georgia
- Hong Kong

Some countries still haven't made up their minds and are still in dilemma regarding the use of Bitcoin. In such cases, the usage of BTC is legal in the sense that you can own it, but there are no clear rules or legal protection concerning its status. These countries are either already creating a legal framework for Bitcoin and cryptocurrencies, or have taken a wait-and-see approach. These "undecided" countries include:

LEGALITY

- Albania
- Andorra
- Argentina
- Barbados
- Colombia
- French Guiana
- Gabon
- Jamaica
- Jordan
- Kazakhstan
- Kenya
- Kosovo
- Kyrgyzstan
- Malaysia
- The Maldives
- Mauritius
- Nigeria
- Panama
- Paraguay
- Peru
- Tunisia
- The United Arab Emirates
- Tanzania
- Uruguay

The legalization of cryptocurrencies doesn't necessarily mean that the government of the particular country is supporting or promoting the virtual currencies in any way.

The Countries which have declared Crypto currency illegal include *Algeria, Bolivia, Ecuador, Bangladesh, Nepal, Macedonia* (as of 2020).

What is Blockchain Technology?

Blockchain is a combination of two words, 'Blocks' and 'Chains', the Blockchain system is a system of recording or storing information in such a way that makes it difficult or nearly impossible to change, cheat or hack into. It is a digital Ledger of transactions that is duplicated, recorder and distributed across the entire network of computer systems which are present in the block chain. Blockchain technology is the stem or the foundation on which the concept of all crypto currencies are based on. 'Block' chain comprises of blocks of information, which are all linked together in a digital chain for the data to get transferred, digital chains are the public database where the information is stored. These blocks which are a part of this digital chain, need to talk to the next block for the data to be transferred from one block to another. Each block in the chain contains a number of transactions, and each time a new transaction occurs on the blockchain, a record of this transaction would be added to the digital ledger of each and every participant. These blocks can literally store all kinds of information from your transaction history, dates, money, time, numbers etc. The decentralised database which is managed by multiple participants is known as the Distributed Ledger Technology, also known as 'DLT'. Blockchain possesses certain sets of characteristics, which include:

1. **Programmable** – A blockchain is programmable and can be made with the help of smart contracts.

2. **Distributed** – All the participants in this network have a copy of the ledger to maintain full or complete transparency.

3. **Secure** – All the transactions which take place are recorded immediately in the Digital ledger and all the records are individually encrypted.

4. **Immutable** – Any records of the transactions which are validated are irreversible and cannot be changed.

5. **Anonymous** – The identity of the participants will always be anonymous or pseudonymous.

6. **Unanimous** – All the participants in the network agree to the validity of each and every records.

7. **Time stamped** – All the transaction time stamps are recorded on the blocks.

For a block of information to be stored in blockchain, certain steps have to be followed, which include:

1. A transaction should take place on the blockchain.

2. The transaction should be verified.
3. The transaction then is to be stored in the form of a block.
4. The block of this transaction should get a unique identification code called a hash generated by nonces.
5. These blocks are then bound and secured together using some cryptographic principles that are called chains.

To make things simpler, and to explain on a lighter note, Blockchain is a series of immutable data blocks. It consists of a cluster of computers which are needed to manage this data series as no central authority is present to manage it. The process of passing information in this series from point A to point B is much more secure, simpler and devoid of any transaction cost. This system decentralises the storage of information as nothing that one feeds into it is ever stored in a single location. The records that are maintained, are completely public and can be easily verified. Moreover, the entire blockchain system is immutable, which means it is impossible for anyone to tamper with the data.

A blockchain consists of a numbers of blocks in the digital chain, if one block in one chain is changed, it would be immediately apparent that it had been tampered or fiddled with. If any hacker or a group of hackers wanted to corrupt a blockchain system, they would have to change every single block in that particular chain, across all of the distributed versions of the chain.

Application of Blockchain Technology

In the case of cybersecurity, there has been no better technology used, as that of the Blockchain system. The general public who may not have curiosity in this field would think that blockchain is all related to Bitcoin and other cryptocurrencies, but such is not the case. It's application is far reached than just to the crypto world.

1. Blockchain system can be used in **Government sector** to ensure the safety of its public records. The government sector has been actively trying to tap the full power and potential which the blockchain technology possess. The largest records of each individual present in a country is stored in a government database and is the perfect hot target for the hackers to vandalise and abuse the system. Protection of these records is very crucial for the government, with the blockchain technology around, blockchain data structures deployed for secure storage of such data, governments can easily harden the network security and prevent any breach or causality. It reduces the single- point- of failure risk and ensures minimum cyber breach in the data.

    Through the means of decentralisation, blockchain can offer more transparency in government operations. It can always ascertain the people that there is zero corruption and they can look into and verify the data anytime they want. Other than this, it is also not feasible for any government to reserve large chunks of resources in this, they need to be efficient and should reduce cost at all costs.

The blockchain system can also be implemented to reduce the redundancies in carrying operations, streamlining it, and decreasing any burden on the audits. It could also speed up the process of reconciling funds and many other government operations.

2. Block chain in **Retail Industry** can be used to eliminate the Third-Party Interference.

    Advancement of technology, being dynamic, has disrupted the retail industry at every turn. While the e- commerce portals transformed everyone into online shoppers, technologies like extended reality, predictive analytics, machine learning, etc., are disrupting the manner in which we shop in the conventional sense. However, going digital did come with its setback and brought online frauds and cheats with it. This is where the e-commerce companies and retail businesses are tapping into blockchain for.

    The big players of the retail industry are tapping on blockchain to secure their operations and make it look more alluring or trust worthy for the shoppers. It can be used to add transparency in the transaction and providing the customers with the complete details about the product right from its date of production to the details of how it can be used.

Many retail businesses are also using blockchain to bring in the future of currencies, cryptocurrencies. Some retailers allow cryptocurrencies as a deposit for hard cash to get more business from across the borders. Customer loyalty programs can be commissioned by retail people using blockchain.

On a different aspect, it can also help eliminate the inefficiencies of logistics and supply chain management in the retail industry.

3. Block chain can be used in in **Financial Service**; To cut back costs and reduce Fees.

Blockchain's potential in financial services is something many professionals have been looking into. In fact, a recent survey report stated that over 91% of the banks worldwide have started investing in blockchain solutions. It could be easily used to make transactions by the financial institutions more secure and efficient. Acting as a ledger, blockchain can be used for recording and storing all the financial transactions without giving any one single point of risk. The data would be stored in multiple locations and a copy of new transactions would be added to each of the ledgers.

In case someone tries to hack or play with the data of financial transactions stored in these ledgers, it would be required to get into each ledger, which would practically be impossible.

Apart from securing these, it can also be used to speed-up the cross-border transactions, increasing transparency in transactions, and allowing digital identity verification.

4. Blockchain in **Health care** to manage Patient database authenticity.

Blockchain technology is also revolutionizing the healthcare and medicine industry. The decentralized system presented by blockchain would break down the central authority for storing the medicine-related data. Transferring of the patient medical records becomes more transparent with blockchain technology. It can encrypt the patient data which can then be used in the times of any harmful disease outbreak, like in the case of COVID-19.

It can also be used for the control of the temperature in which the pharmaceutical products should be stored to maintain the potency. This blockchain technology can then also be effective in tracking and tracing the shipment of the medicines, so that the customer knows the exact whereabouts of the product. When doing clinical trials, doctors can also transfer files including patient data, payer information, etc., through the encrypted system of blockchain. By the use of smart contracts, blockchain technology can also be used for connecting patients with healthcare to provide value-based healthcare.

Many companies are even using blockchain to counter drug scams through traceability and knowing any counterfeits, in addition to this it can tell about falsified medicines.

Blockchain used in **Real Estate** solves Land registry problems. Blockchain has started disrupting the real estate marketing of different countries across the globe. It is certainly acting as the flag-bearer of digital transformation for this sector. Its decentralized technology for record-keeping would help to instil a level of trust among the buyers of the property. Whether it is property purchase, title management, conducting due diligence on the property or even getting crowd-sourced investment, blockchain would enable it all.

Blockchain-based property management software and other tools would be used by real estate giants to keep the ledger. The peer-to-peer network platform offered by the decentralized technology would help in putting an end to corruption and fraudulence in this sector.

It can allow property to be listed on a single decentralized blockchain database to ensure that the reliable data for listed properties is provided to the customer or buyers for financial valuation of the property and tracking the history while avoiding any third-party contact. It also provides a more transparent and quick mode for payment without involving any intermediaries.

What is Hashing?

Blockchain in itself is a type of DLT (Distributed Ledger Technology) in which transactions are recorded with an immutable cryptographic signature which is known as 'Hash'.

Block chain works by including the identifier of the last block into the identifier of the following block to create an unbreakable and immutable digital chain. To make the addition of more and more blocks being added to the chain and to keep the blockchain data manageable and secure, an algorithm is present which is called 'Hashing'. This Hashing, works in combination with a consolidating data structure known as *Merkle Tree*.

When a transaction has been verified and is in process to be added to a particular block in a digital chain, it will put through a hash algorithm to convert it into a set of unique numbers and letters, which is similar to the creation of password by a random password generator. After this, two transaction hashes will be combined and put through the hash algorithm again to produce another unique hash. This process of combining multiple transactions into new hashes continues until finally there remains only one hash, which is considered to be the 'root' hash of several transactions. The unique nature of Hash and one of the key security feature for the Blockchains, is that they only work in one way and there is no alternative method to do so. The same data being used will end up producing the same hash of numbers and letters, it is impossible to 'un-hash', or reverse the process, using the numbers and letters to convert or decipher the original data.

Merkle Tree

The hashing process which is done using the exact same transactions, will always end up producing the same hashes. This feature allows anyone who uses the blockchain to check that the data has not been tampered with, because any change in any part of the data will result in a completely different hash, which will in return effect each and every iteration of hashes all the way, down to the root. This concept is known as the Merkle Tree. It also fulfils the purpose of significantly reducing the amount of data which is required to be stored and transmitted or broadcast over the network by summarising sets of hashed transactions into a single root hash. As each of this transaction is hashed, then combined and hashed again, the final root hash will be of a standard size.

ICO (INITIAL COIN OFFERING)

Initial Coin Offering (ICO) is a newly introduced method of crowdfunding which businesses, especially the cryptocurrency start-ups, are using to raise funds for their new projects in order to launch their own cryptocurrencies. In simpler terms, ICO is an event through which a cryptocurrency company releases and sells its tokens with the purpose to raise funds.

The steps to start an ICO are very simple, the developer has to start the ICO campaign, the market makers then purchase a share of IOU and deposit it to the coin for which the ICO is being held. Traders can then buy their share of the coin, IOUs are then transformed into tokens which are available for deposit/withdrawal.

The said company is to announce a new crypto-token and sells its future tokens to interested buyers and investors in exchange for fiat currency, Bitcoins, or any other cryptocurrency.

ICO is a proven way of raising funds to initiate a crypto project, however, the success of the project depends on a number of things, including the concept, demand, technology, and the team.

Short Guide to Start an ICO

Launching an ICO can be easy and very tempting, but to make it successful is the most difficult part. The steps include-

1. **Research** – To start your ICO, you should have a proper research model that your coin will add value to the society at the point which you are introducing it. Before a person plans to launch a cryptocurrency, he should have all the possible knowledge about the basic dynamics and working of the crypto currency and the industry.

2. **Eligibility** – A person who wants to launch his ICO should be aware of the basic requirements to qualify the eligibility criteria of the ICO. The coin should focus on providing value to the users, should be authentic and provide absolute transparency. Also, how will the introduction of this crypto impact the lives of users or what product can be linked to this.

3. **Problem solving** – The factor on which the coin of a developer should be depended upon is having a problem solving nature. The developers should realise that what is the need

of the hour and at that point of time what is the demand of the market and the public.

If a person is planning to create a crypto just for the sole purpose of trading and earning money, he should think more than twice as the core concept to crypto and blockchain is not to trade and gamble money. Even if the coin holds a good price at the start eventually it will crash and fail when people will come to know that there is no true potential in it(just like DOGECOIN, which I will discuss in the latter part of the book). The real test of stability will begin only at the end of the ICO, when the true potential of the coin will come into play, as if the demand is up then the price will go up and if the demand falls the price will also end up falling and the value of the coin will go down.

4. **Goal oriented approach** – During the process of development of the project, the following should be communicated to the target audience-

   1. The team members who will be working on this project.

   2. The purpose or the goal which one is achieving through this ICO.

   3. The methodology by which the developers will ensure the protection of the interests and money of the investors.

5. **Teamwork** – In order to pull the ICO off for a long term purpose and to add substantive value to the coin, team work is the most essential

part of this process. Choice of the team should be made very wisely, the teammates must be qualified to be a part of this project and should only be the people that one trusts and believes in. The investors and buyers would have a keen interest about the team which is behind this project. Details of the team members with their photos should be present on the official page of the coin, this will help in building a trustworthy relation between the customers and the coin nexus. It is also recommended to have high-level professional advisors as a part of your team as they can guide the project through the long run.

6. **Creation of Quality White Paper** – Whitepapers are the documents which tells a buyer or a potential buyer everything that there is to know about the projects, which includes the idea which one stands for, long term goal, the value which the coin is providing, user benefits, information about the ICO, investor options, technical aspects, roadmap to the future towards which it is working. The goals of the project should be defined in a realistic and well defined manner so that it is clear to the target audience, otherwise the buyers will think that the goals are unclear and the team does not actually know what it is doing.

7. **Extra measures for investor terms** – Your investors will always like and appreciate if you will take extra measures in order to protect

their investments. In order to do so, it is suggested to establish good escrow wallets to protect the funds, good offerings of discount and premiums, also to create a mechanism to return the funds if the project fails.

8. **Some other factors** – The time during which one is launching the ICO should be apt for his concept, as the availability should be made during the demand of the product. While introducing the project, the entire team should be actively promoting the coin on social media, as good PR and Marketing strategies are a must in order to spread the word and create the hype.

   It is important to hire ICO developers, website developers, marketers, white paper writers etc. It is important to not break any kind of law and to maintain user trust at all costs.

Some of the cryptos, which the society is widely talking about are mentioned below, the description of these cryptos are purely based on my research, analysis and experience in the Crypto market.

BITCOIN

In the past several years, many attempts have been made for creating a digital currency or digital money, but have always ended up failing. The main reason for the failure is trust. Bitcoin was designed to solve this problem by the use of a specific type of data base called a blockchain. Most of the normal databases which are used regularly, always have someone in charge who can change the entries, abusing the powers at any point of time and could wrongly use it for their own advantage, therefore, Blockchain is different as there is no in charge of the Blockchain system, it is run by the people who use it, it was formed to avoid this human error in the transactions. Blockchain is to Bitcoin what the Internet is to E-mail. The crypto currencies such as bitcoin can't be faked, hacked or even double spent, so people that own this money can always trust that it has some value to it.

Bitcoin is considered as the first ever cryptocurrency to have been ever created where, a group of programmers got together with a pseudo name called 'Satoshi Nakamoto', who raised this thought provoking question "Why do we need a bank or a third party for two different people in order to pay each other?". Why do we have to or need to trust a third party for a transaction which is being taken place between two independent parties, using the mode of exchange which they would feel comfortable with, i.e. the preferred currency. To counter this problem, the idea of the mechanism was first created and termed as 'Bitcoin', so that there is no need for a bank or government or even an organisation to regulate and carry out the process which an individual carries out in his day to day life.

If a person holds bitcoin he has two keys, one is the public key, the other is the private key. A public key is just like an email address which you can give to anyone, so that the peer can send the person a bitcoin on the other hand the private key is more like a password to your email, you should not give it away to anyone and protect it at all costs. There is no option to reset the pass for the private key, for instance if you do not remember the pass to the private key, your bitcoins will never come back to you as you have lost them, there is no option to reset or change or form a new private key for the same.

The Bitcoin is limited in number, and there are only 21 million bitcoins in this world, that is the reason why it is referred to as digital gold. It is estimated that the last bitcoin ever to be, would be mined in the year 2100.

The most widely asked question by the common people is that "Where does this bitcoin come from?"

The answer to this is that new bitcoins are generate by a competitive and decentralised process which is called *mining*. Mining for the crypto currencies can be referred to as digging for oil or gold. The people who use supercomputers to solve really complex equations and get rewarded bitcoin in return are referred to as miners. These Puzzles or equations keep on getting more difficult as more and more people try to solve it, whoever solves it first gets rewarded with some amount of bitcoins. The amount of bitcoin which the miners can actually win by solving these puzzles, decreases over the period of time, this is the main reason why more and more people hold or HODL(Hold for Dear LIFE) the bitcoin. When the availability of bitcoins decreases and more people keep on holding to it, the price of the Bitcoin starts escalating, similarly, when more and more people sell the bitcoin it leads to more availability in the market, therefore the price starts to drop down. Seeing the current scenario the value of the bitcoin is increasing hour by hour and day by day, therefore the people are getting driven or motivated to invest whatever they have in this crypto. Bitcoin can also be transferred from one person to the other which is known as Peer to Peer transaction. This transaction is so fast that it gets completed within a fraction of seconds, at times even in a millisecond.

The value that a Bitcoin possesses is considerably huge only for the reason that people are holding it. It adds to the uniqueness to the coin as people think that it is a store of value and cannot be replicated easily and is rare. Bitcoin has now, to some extent become a value for which goods and services can be traded which has even more escalated the price charts of bitcoin. The logic is really simple, if people think and believe that a commodity is valuable, then it surely is valuable. For the purpose of buying bitcoin, you do not necessarily buy the entire bitcoin, you can always end up buying some amount of a bitcoin. One bitcoin can be broken down to 8 decimal points which is known as one 'Satoshi'.

The requirements to mine bitcoins on your own includes a powerful computer, a powerful GPU, and an Application Specific Integrated Circuit (ASIC). ASICS are silicon chips which are designed for a very specific purpose, they are created to perform a repeated function very effectively as opposed to the General purpose chips which can perform an endless variety of functions, but are comparatively less efficient. The electricity consumption which is used for the purpose of mining a bitcoin is also very huge. One has to be calculative during the mining process because if the investment made for mining is near about the same for the outcome value it is mining then it is a waste of time and resources. If the system is really powerful and the hash rate or mining rate is really good only then it is beneficial to mine a bitcoin.

Who was SATOSHI NAKAMOTO?

In the year 2009, when the bitcoin was created nobody really knew what it was. The knowledge about this industry and the Bitcoin was so less, that a guy named *Laszlo Hanyecz* had ordered a Papa John's pizza and paid for it by using 10,000 of his bitcoins.

The story of Bitcoin starts with just a name 'Satoshi Nakamoto', behind this name is really a shadow, a ghost that nobody actually knows of. This name has a lot of conspiracy theories behind it which piques and stirs our imagination. He is that spectre who had put his name on the domain called 'bitcoin.org' on 18 August, 2008, he then wrote a paper which was titled as 'Bitcoin: A Peer-to-Peer Electronic Cash System', and after hanging around for a couple more years, he was gone.

Nobody really knows who actually is Satoshi Nakamoto, but in 2012, an extremely intelligent guy from Japan, who was 37 years old, claimed to be Satoshi. No one actually believed it back then and now one actually believes it now, after a considerable amount of research and being involved in the industry for quite a long time, it would be fair to say that this could not have been done by a single person, therefore Satoshi Nakamoto may actually be a group of people who created the bitcoin. A long while ago, famous tech entrepreneur John McAfee claimed that he actually knows who the Bitcoin wizard, Satoshi is but he will not reveal it, which was considered to be outlandish by the entire world.

An Internet Security Researcher called Dan Kaminsky, tried to unmask this Japanese Genius a while ago, he had informed the *New Yorker* that he knew one thing for sure and that Satoshi was a world class programmer, with a deep understanding of C++ programming language, he has profound knowledge about economics, cryptography and peer to peer networking. Dan strongly believed that this project was made by a group of people as only an out of the world genius can pull this off.

Speculations were quite a times made that Satoshi can probably be a Finnish tech researcher and programmer *Vili Lehdonvirta*, but that was really unlikely because when this was brought to his notice, it was clear that he did not know cryptography that well and surely he would have given his day job at the university where he was currently working at.

Another such speculation was made about *Gavin Andresen*, who was the guy who took over bitcoin after Nakamoto disappeared. Gavin once said that he did know who Nakamoto was and he was the one who gave the name *Craig Wright,* but this was only because Wright had claimed that he was Satoshi. This became controversial when he was investigated and it was found that either he actually created this or he is a really good liar, because it is said that he wrote some messages using cryptographic keys that were inextricably linked to blocks of Bitcoin created by the Nakamoto. He even registered a US copyright for Bitcoin 0.1, but the US copyright office said that the copyright does not actually mean much. Even though Wright's claim was supported by a lot of other people, the *Wired* in an interview stated that either he created the bitcoin or he is a brilliant hoaxer who desperately wants the people to believe him, Wright has even threatened a lot of people to sue for libel who say that it wasn't him who created it.

In 2019, he dropped a bombshell saying that Satoshi Nakamoto was not only him, but he lead a team of brilliant people, in which he was the principal actor and the other people involved in this were *Dave Kleinman* and *Hai Finney*.

Kleinman was an avid cryptographer, who is not alive anymore, he passed away back in 2013, he was on the mailing list of this Nakamoto character, and was quite skilled at the arts of building encryption-focused software. But, according to the experts the only evidence that he was a part of this team was the claim made by Craig Wright. It is believed that Kleinman died in poverty, his body was found decomposing and surrounded by empty alcohol bottles and a loaded handgun, a bullet hole was also found in his mattress, though no spent shell casings were found at the scene. This is where the story get weirder, allegedly Kleinman died with a massive stack of Bitcoin, after this people started to believe that Kleinman alone was Nakamoto. Also, his brother has not released his hard drives, which could have some really valuable information.

Hal Finney, was said to be a pre- bitcoin cryptographic pioneer. He was considered to be a genius and if he wasn't actually Nakamoto, the two could be said to endowed with similar intellectual properties. Bitcoin.com had earlier written that Hal epitomises Bitcoin more than any other known person. The writing experts claim that Finney and Nakamoto had a very similar handwriting, but same was the case with Adresen too. It is also believed that he was a ghost writer for Nakamoto, not that he was the man himself, but Finney denied being Nakamoto and even let the investigators inside his house, and it was later concluded that he was telling the truth. There is no doubt that Finney and Nakamoto were in constant contact to each other via email, people claim that if Nakamoto was trying to hide that why is it that Finney was openly mailing Nakamoto, or the reason could be that Finney is Nakamoto in a disguise.

Finney was the first guy to ever receive a Bitcoin transaction from Nakamoto, unfortunately Finney got a disease called the ALS, known as Lou Gehrig's disease and became paralysed which eventually lead to his death in 2014.

It is considered that these three people were surely present at the beginning of the bitcoin, another strange addition to this story is that a man who lived down the street from Finner was called *Dorian Nakamoto*. He was also a computer whiz and a libertarian, in 2014 he got investigated by a news week journal and he said "I am no longer involved in that and I cannot discuss it. It's been turned over to other people, they are in charge of it now, I no longer have any connection". Later Dorian stated that he had misunderstood the question and thought that the journalist was talking about his military work, which was classified and he was not allowed to talk about it to anyone.

After this, something strange started to happen, the real Nakamoto's P2P Foundation account came alive for the first time in 5 years and a message read "I am not Dorian Nakamoto. Some people believed that it was hacked, the others believe that even though he may be part of classified defence projects and also a computer engineer for technology and financial information services, but he certainly does not have enough brains to be the real Nakamoto, unless he hid his super intelligence really well.

Nick Szabo was another name which comes up a lot when talking about Nakamoto, because he certainly did have the brain power to create something like Bitcoin, the reason for this is that he published a paper on 'Bit Gold', which was a theoretical decentralised currency which never actually got into work but was certainly a precursor to Bitcoin. He had envisioned and laid out a plan like Bitcoin before Bitcoin even came out. He was no doubt considered as a certified genius and the investigators have even said that he was Nakamoto as he was the only one who could actually know how to create something like the Bitcoin, One investigator wrote that, "I've concluded that there is only one person in the whole world that has the sheer breadth but also specific knowledge and it is this chap". There is also evidence on one of his blogs that he wrote about intending to invent a real life version of his BitGold.

Szabo, strongly denies that he is Nakamoto, but has admitted that if anyone in this world who he knew of, were to create the technology of Bitcoin, it would've been him or Finner or a guy called Wei Dai. He says that he has immense respect for Nakamoto, as Satoshi came along and improved a number of aspects of it and made it even more trust minimised and smooth to function. Szabo, along with the entire world still do not have an idea about who Nakamoto really was. Right now Satoshi Nakamoto is still a missing person, and is considered *Keyser Söze* of cryptocurrencies.

ETHEREUM

The second largest crypto currency to be around is *Ethereum*. Ethereum was first proposed in in the year 2013 and then was brought to life in 2014 by *Vitalik Buterin*. Vitalik at that time was the co-founder of the Bitcoin Magazine. Ethereum is the do it yourself platform for decentralised programs also known as Dapps (Decentralised Apps). If you want to create a decentralised program that no single person controls, not even you, who actually wrote it, you just have to learn the Ethereum programming Language which is known as *Solidity* and begin coding. The Ethereum Platform has thousands of independent computers running it, which means it is fully decentralised. Once a program is deployed to the Ethereum network tense computers, also known as nodes, will make sure it executes as written. Ethereum is basically the infrastructure for running DApps worldwide. It's not a currency, it's a platform, which has a goal to truly decentralize the Internet. The currency which is used to incentivize the network is called Ether. Almost all activities on the web has an involvement of a third party or an intermediary, Bitcoin showed the world a whole new array of opportunities by decentralised digital network.

Ethereum connects the people directly through a powerful decentralised super computer, it is a network of computers that together combine into one powerful, decentralised supercomputer.

Solidity, which is a coding language of Ethereum, is used to write 'Smart Contracts', which are the logic that runs DApps. Real life contacts are a set of "Ifs" and "Thens", which means that they are a set of conditions and actions, Similarly, Ethereum developers write the conditions for their program or DApp and then the Ethereum network executes it. They are known as Smart contracts because they deal with all of the aspects of the contract which are enforcement, management, performance and payment.

The downside of these kind of contracts are that they are self-executing and are different from Intelligent contracts. An Intelligent contract takes into account a lot of factors if the contract terms are not being fulfilled such as, extenuating circumstances, the spirit with which the contract was written and it would also be able to make exceptions if warranted. In simpler words it would act as a really good judge. The concept of Smart contract is different from that of an Intelligent contract. It is uncompromisingly letter strict, it follows the rules down to a T and it does not take any secondary considerations or the "spirit" of the law into account just like that in the case of real world contracts. Also, once a smart contract is deployed on the Ethereum network, it can never be edited or corrected, even by the original author, therefore it is immutable. The only way to change this contract would be to convince the entire Ethereum Network that a change should be made and that's virtually impossible. This problem is really serious, as unlike Bitcoin, this platform was created to help create really complex contracts and complex contracts are very difficult to secure. The more complex the nature of the contract, the harder it is to enforce it, as more room is left for interpretations or more clauses must be written in order to deal with contingencies, with the use of smart contract, security mean handling with perfect accuracy every possible way in which a contract can be executed, in order to make sure that the contract does only what its writer or creator intended it to do.

Ethereum launched an idea of "Code is Law", which means that a contract on Ethereum is the ultimate authority and nobody could over rule the contract. This mental bubble of the platform popped after the DAO event took place. DAO stands for Decentralised Autonomous organisation which allowed the users to deposit their money and get their returns on the investments which were made by DAO. On the other hand, the decisions would be decentralised and crowdsourced. DAO successfully raised 150 Million $ in Ethereum currency, that is Ether, when Ether was trading around 20$. While this all sounded very good the code wasn't secured very well and resulted in someone figuring out a way to drain the DAO out of money. It was believed that the person who did this had found loopholes in the DAO's smart contract. After this incident the Ethereum community decided that the "Code is no longer the law" and changed the Ethereum rules, in order to revert all the money that went in the DAO. The Ethereum developers decided to bail the investors and the contract writers because of which this happened, but, the small minority that didn't agree with the move stuck to the Ethereum blockchain before it's protocol was altered, which lead to the birth of the Ethereum Classic, which is the original Ethereum. Ethereum uses 'proof of work', although it is gradually moving to 'proof of stake' with the Ethereum 2.0.

Ether, was first distributed in Ethereum's original Initial Coin Offering, in 2014 at the price of 0.40$.

RIPPLE (XRP)

Ripple was created by Ripple Labs, the idea was first ever conceived by Ryan Fugger back in 2004 and was known as Ripplepay, but in 2012 it was passed to *Jed McCaleb* and *Chris Larsen*, who were the founders of 'Open Coin', which later came to be known as Ripple Labs. Ripple, with the help of a protocol called Ripplenet or (RTXP), are trying to move value around the world while aiming to create 'Internet of Value', which is a way for money to move as quickly as an information does.

With the use of this technology there is no need to wait for days and even pay a hefty amount while transferring money globally.

Unlike most cryptocurrencies in the industry who have their focus on the individual, Ripple Labs aim to serve banks and payment providers, allowing them to lower the transaction costs and expedite settlements.

Ripple is not a centralised crypto but the Ripple Labs do maintain it.

Ripple Net is a network which is based on certain rules, known as the Ripple transaction protocol or RTXP. This network consist of computers known as validators, that are spread around the entire world and maintain a shared ledger of the who owns what. It is the duty of validators to make sure that every transaction sent through the network follows the RTXP rules. Anyone can run a validator and help maintain the Ripple network, exactly like anyone can run a Bitcoin node to maintain the Bitcoin network. Companies who want to access the Ripple Network can use gateways, which are usually used by banks, act as entry points to Ripple for people outside the network. It's just the same as visiting a bank or a credit company to gain access to the banking system. Ripple offers businesses an alternative to the banking system in the form of an Internet of value called the Ripple net.

xRapid, *xVia* and *xCurrent* are all Ripple products which are offered to the companies in order to optimise their current solution for transferring money around the world. This solution is absolutely for all the customers of financial services using Ripple, if the banks start using this technology then everybody's bank account balance would be residing on the XRP ledger. Unlike other cryptocurrency protocols which supports only their own assets, Ripple offers two different types of currencies i.e. I*OUs* and the *XRP*.

IOUs are tokens that can be stored in any Ripple Wallet, it does not represent something that one owns, it represents debt or something which one owes. Issuing of IOU to someone means that the issuer owes the other person something, holding an IOU means that the other individual owes you something. Each IOU comprises of a name based on who issued it and what it represents, it can be issued for any type of real world asset and a new IOU is to be issued every time an asset is borrowed. IOU for the same types of asset are not interchangeable if they are issued by two different people. Each IOU has a different credit line or trust line, it in itself is no asset, it's just a promise by the issuer to give you the asset back in the future. The promise would not have much value if the issuer isn't true to his words, therefore IOUs run on the principle of trust.

In the RippleNet there is a line known as the Trust line, which is quite similar to the line of credit with the bank, it is an agreement to trust someone up to a limited amount of money.

The *XRP* is another currency which is supported by the Ripple protocol. Issued by Ripple Labs, this currency helps to transfer payments through the Ripple network. Unlike the IOU, XRP is a type of payment which is final and is considered as a tradeable asset by anyone on the network. XRP is considered as an actual asset and not a liability. Even though XRPs are fast and scalable they are considered to be volatile and also is not respected worldwide. It takes just 4 seconds to send and XRP transaction through the network, on the other hand Bitcoin takes up to 10 minutes to do so. Other than this XRP can handle 1,500 transactions per second, while Bitcoin can only handle 7 transactions.

XRP cannot be mined ad mining in the case of bitcoin is done in order to confirm and determine the order of transactions on the blockchain. In the case of Ripple transactions are handled in a different scenario. XRP transactions are broadcast through the network, the validators who are maintaining the network decide it's validity, by the process of voting. When a validator receives a transaction, it consults with the other validators and they altogether vote on whether the transaction is valid or not, if 80% of the validators voted 'Valid' then it is updated in the Ripple ledger. This list of trusted validators that a validator consults with is known as UNL or Unique Node List, each validator has its own UNL. Deciding that who will be included in the validator's UNL is completely upto the person who runs the validator, however Ripple offers a default list of trusted validators. Validators don't actually get compensated for their work as that in the case of the Bitcoins and miners.

About 100 Billion XRPs have been pre-mined and there can be no more XRPs ever, out of which 20 Billion XRP were given to the founders of Ripple, *Jed Macaleb, Chris Larsen* and *Arthur Britto*, 7 Billion XRP is held by the Ripple Labs, more than 40 Billions XRPs have been sold to companies and individuals and the remaining supply is sealed in a smart contract, which releases 1 billion XRP every month in the Ripple labs, until all of the 100 Billion XRP cap will be reached.

XRP can be broken up to 6 decimal points, and the smallest unit is known as a 'Drop'. A wallet is needed in order to store the XRO and a minimum deposit of 20 XRP should be there in your account, this is done to prevent people to spam the Ripple network by creating a large number of accounts. As time passes XRP will keep getting more valuable as it is limited in supply.

LITECOIN

Litecoin is a peer to peer cryptocurrency which originally an early spinoff of bitcoin or an altcoin. It is an open source software project released under the MIT/X11 license. It is a global payment network which is completely decentralised and has no involvement of central authorities. Mathematics secures the network and empowers individuals to control their own finances. Litecoin has faster transaction confirmation times and has an improved storage efficiency compared to the leading math based currency. Litecoin has gained a substantial industry support, trade volume and liquidity in the past years and is proven medium of commerce which is similar or even complimentary to Bitcoin.

It was created by Charlie Lee in October 2011, and the creator aimed at creating a lighter version of Bitcoin for the purpose of everyday transactions.

There were three major things which the Litecoin or the LTC brought to the table; faster transactions, cheaper transactions and more decentralisation.

Being an open source project LTC ensures security as anyone can review the codes and suggest improvements. New transactions on average are added to the blockchain in every 2.5 minute, which is quite a reasonable time to wait for payments., as Bitcoin takes 10 minutes. The Litecoin was the first cryptocurrency to adopt the Lightning Network, in May, 2017 the first ever Lightning Network transaction took place on a Litecoin, sending 0.00000001 LTC or 1 photon, which is the smallest fraction of LTC from Zurich to San Frransisco in just under 1 second.

The Lightning Network is layer-2 network which is built on top of the actual blockchain that facilitates instant and practically fee-less transactions between two parties and it can even scale to support millions of transaction per second. The LTC blockchain supports 54 transactions per second, that is like a tortoise compared to an aeroplane. LTC is considered to be more decentralised than the Bitcoin, as it uses a different Proof-of-Work algorithm called *Scrypt*. The value which the LTC derives comes from the cost to mine LTC, which means the comparatively lower cost of the mining equipment than Bitcoin, but it mainly depends on the electricity which the equipment consumes. Also, the coin is scarce in number and does have a limited supply which increases its value, only 84 million LTC will ever be created and if you know that central banks can print as much money as they wish, similar is not the case with LTC.

People who think LTC is or will be valuable in future, their demand facilitate the rates at which it is being sold, as the demand for it constantly increases. Bitcoin is considered to be 'Digital Gold' on the other hand LTC acts as its counterpart 'Digital Silver'.

Dogecoin

Dogecoin is a cryptocurrency which started as a joke or a meme that somehow became a real crypto currency. It was introduced on December 6, 2013, Jackson Palmer who was a self-identified 'average geek, who made fun of the amount of altcoins present in the industry, so even he along with Billy Markus create a payment system disguised as a fun joke or meme.

The Dogecoin features the face of the Shiba Inu, which is a dog from the meme 'Doge', as its logo and also the title. This joke blew so out of proportion that it developed its own online community which lead it to a market capitalisation of $ 5,382,875,000 on January 28, 2021.

Dogecoin is an altcoin which has many users, the meme has been so popular now that from nothing, it actually is being used for doing certain online payments. Trading of physical, tangible items in exchange for DOGE takes place on online communities such as *Reddit* and *Twitter*, where the users frequently share information related to this Altcoin.

The hype around it is so much that it has also been used to try to sell a house, it has also been used in poker industry and pornographic industry.

Dogetipbot was a transaction service used on social media sites like *Reddit* and *Twitch*, it allowed the users to send Dogecoins to each other through commands via Reddit comments. In the year 2017, Dogetipbot was discontinued and taken offline after its creator was declared as bankrupt, this let a lot of Dogetipbot users losing their coins stored in Dogetipbot system.

In February, 2014 Palmer announced that the limit of the Dogecoins would be removed in order to create a consistent reduction of its inflation rate over the period of time.

The recent boost to this hype was given by *Elon musk* and some other reddit users which led to an increase in 800% of the price of this crypto. The constant tweets of Elon musk has hugely influenced the market of Dogecoin, but there is still speculation about his support being a joke, as he is known for his trolls on twitter, or is he actually a supporter and is vouching for it.

Due to so much hype around it might be no surprise if doge coin becomes one of the main stream medium of transactions online, rumours also say that Jeff Bezos is also planning to accept this mode for the payments in amazon. But these are just speculations or guesses and there is no truth in it as of now, this will only be clear in the coming times ahead.

TRON

In the year 2014, Justin Sun founded Tron and caught the eyes of the investors in 2017, it raised $ 70 Million in the same year by its ICO, shortly before China outlawed the Digital tokens. Tron or the TRX is ranked in the top 20 coins by the market cap. Tron aims at decentralising the web by building an infrastructure of smart contracts and decentralised apps in order to enable the future of the internet, or what Tron calls, Web 4.0. Web4 is an internet which is without any middlemen or third party intermediaries like content gatekeepers or media conglomerates. In this web or future, the creators can create content freely without centralised services and reach their consumers directly in a Peer to Peer way.

Tron took over Steemit, a decentralised social media platform with over 10,000 active users in February 2020. As the world of DeFi is continuing to explode, Tron DeFi will not be left behind. It launched the Tron based Decentralised Exchange Polonidex and the Just Network, which is made up of the stablecoin JUST STABLE, a lending protocol JUST LEND, and an oracle service called the JUST LINK.

TRX is slowly tapping into the gaming world as well, it has shown interests in games like Aftermath

Islands, Crypto Dungeons and Score Milk, all of which has created enormous utility for the TRX coin, which is the main network token powering all transactions and applications on the Tron Blockchain. Tron TRX is used in several ways such as granting the stakers with voting rights, issuing other DApp tokens on Tron, and it is also used as a cryptocurrency to trade and make payments while being stored in the Tron wallet.

Tron's estimation of total transaction volume in October 2020 generated $280 million.

Tron is widely been compared to Ethereum and both are given comparisons like the leading smartphone companies of the world, Justin Sun has said that Ethereum is like iPhone and TRX is like android of the crypto world. He even predicted in that in near future TRX will end up having a bigger market share than Ethereum just like Android did.

Tron uses delegated proof of stake as the hashing algorithm and it successfully does 2 thousand transactions per second. It confirms 3 blocks per second in comparison to Ethereum which confirms 1 block every 15 seconds. Tron uses java, python programming languages and the transaction fees of Tron are also free, which is useful for using Tether on Tron, which is a US dollar backed stablecoin. Tron employs a delegated Proof of Stake consensus mechanism with 27 rotating super representatives which act as the validators to the network. All these characteristics make Tron an immensely scalable network, it also has a very strong foothold in the Asian markets with backing from well-heeled investors. Tron was established in Singapore and it has recently announced a partnership with the South Korean tech giant Samsung, which will help distribute Tron-based DApps and token to Samsung's worldwide economy.

BITTORRENT

BitTorrent, is the largest Peer to Peer file sharing protocol with over 100 million users, which was acquired by Tron in July, 2018 for $140 million. In the year 2015, it was estimated that BitTorrent consumed 20% of all broadband traffic of the world. BitTorrent facilitates Peer to Peer file sharing, the users act as seeds for particular files and peers can connect to the network and download for these seeds, this is the original function and the protocol followed by the BTT. With the tokenization of the network there are a whole host of other features which are being planned, one of which is the BitTorrent speed. It is designed to use financial incentives on the BitTorrent network, Peers will now be able to make payments in BTT to increase their positions in download cues and speed up the download process. Seeds are the recipient of these payments which makes them more willing to keep their files online for seeding longer than they might otherwise. This is not the only use of the BTT token, there are some others planned which includes a content delivery system where users advertise their bids and pay BTT to receive content faster, a storage platform where the users can pay for additional storage or get paid to even offer the additional storage and finally a proxy service where users with unreliable internet connectivity can pay the client to retrieve content by URL. The long term goal is to opensource a BTT protocol so that other developers can build additional features on it.

The BTT token was issues on top of the Tron blockchain which makes it a TRC-10 token, it was sold in a Binance launchpad, with its ICO in January, the sale was pretty successful and it manged to conclude it in less than15 minutes. In total the sales saw an evaluation of $7.2 million, which is on top of the $20 million private sale which they had completed prior to it.

Once they were issued BTT started to trade in the aftermarket, prices have been really volatile, which makes sense because of the broader crypto market moves.

BitTorrent will benefit a lot from the star power of Justin Sun who is the face of BTT and TRX both. The Tron team and the Tron community will both help BTT to grow and even push the adoption of BTT and increase the demand.

Cardano (ADA)

Cardano was a project which was started in the year 2015, and has grabbed a lot of attention in the users. It aims in creating an Internet of blockchains, the jump in the price since its beginning which was 2 cents to now, being more than a dollar has caught the eye of the users.

Cardano and Ada are two different things, Cardano is a blockchain while on the other hand ADA is a cryptocurrency that resides on the Cardano blockchain. In simpler words Cardano is a home to the cryptocurrency named ADA, and Cardano can be used to send and receive ADA, it also hosts smart contracts and applications. It has similar working as that of the Ethereum, therefore it is also popular by the name 'Ethereum Killer'. ADA doesn't simply live in the Cardano blockchain, it is a Proof of Stake coin that fuels the Cardano, its purpose is to provide a quick and secure transfer of value and to allow the users to operate smart contracts and applications. The supply of the ADA coins is limited to 45 billion and no further, and the current circulating supply is of 31 billion in ADA coins.

On the entry of new coins in the ecosystem the nodes validate transactions through a consensus algorithm called Ouroboros Proof of Stake. In this type of protocol, nodes who earn a position as slot leaders generate new blocks in the Blockchain and verify the transactions. The Cardano slot leaders in the scenario perform functions much like the Bitcoin miners do. Any person who holds ADA can be a stakeholder and become a slot leader. On becoming a slot leader, you can publish new blocks to the network when Cardano's consensus algorithm selects a coin that you hold. A node is then selected to generate or mint a new block with a probability proportional to the amount of coins that the node has. If a node has any amount of ADA stakes, it will be called the stakeholder. If a node eventually becomes chosen to mint a new block then it is termed as 'Slot leader'. This simply mean that the more Cardano one holds, the greater the opportunity is to become a slot leader and receive rewards.

Cardano is being developed in two layers, this layered architecture is one of the key features that makes Cardano unique. First, is the Cardano Settlement Layer which acts as the balance ledger and runs the transfer of ADA tokens, the other layer is the Cardano Computation Layer which contains in the information on why the transactions occur in the first place, it is this layer which runs the Cardano smart contracts. The two layers separate the ledge of account values from the reason why values are moved from one account to that of the other. Ada can therefore be transferred from one account to another without the information without the information of smart contracts going along for the ride, because the separation enables more flexibility for Cardano smart contracts. Since the computation layer is detached from the settlement layer, users of the computation layer can create rules to filter transactions based on the parameters which they set. Such as a permissioned ledger that excludes transactions that do not include the identification data, which is one of the things that will become more important as blockchain regulation continues to increase. Another key feature which the Cardano has is the interoperability of blockchains, its vision is to create internet of blockchains, which is an ecosystem where Bitcoins can flow into Ethereum and Ripple can flow into Litecoin. One way through which Cardano wants to do this is by the implementation of Sidechains. Sidechains, would enable cross chain transfers without any middlemen, Cardano supports these sidechains based on a new protocol called the KMZ sidechain.

The KMZ sidechain protocol allows the funds to move securely from the computation layer to any blockchain which is using the same protocol. With this protocol, ledgers with certain regulatory compliances are able to interact with the settlement layer without having to share the data, which needs to remain private. Cardano founder, Charles Hoskinson has said that there are over 100 commercial projects lined up in the pipeline.

MATIC NETWORK

Matic network was founded by three Indian developers, Anurag Arjun, Sandeep Naliwal, Jayanti Kanani. All three of them were an active members of India's Bitcoin community, which was relatively small because of the country has a heavy handed approach for the crypto market. Sandeep in one of his interviews explained that India's hostility towards crypto currency has to do with the country's black market economy, which is so large that it would put India into the top 3 largest economy of the world. For this reason many developers are not likely to get involved in the crypto industry in India, especially after the Central Bank of India put a ban on providing banking services to crypto companies. However, the trio was inspired by a technical paper written by Ethereum's founder Vitalik Buterin and developer Joseph Poon, which detailed a scaling solution called the plasma. The very next year, Jayanti Kanani worked with the developers at *Decentraland* to create a more efficient version of the Plasma which was called the more viable plasma, something which is considered to be a huge milestone in the Ethereum space. More viable Plasma gradually became the bedrock for Matic's own technology. The Matic team hosted and attended a number of

Hackathons and crypto currency events around the world, in order to draw more attention to the project, throughout the years 2018 and 2019. All of this paid off when in 2019 the Binance approached the Matic team at one of these events and even offered to fund the project via the Binance launchpad in early 2019. The Matic team accepted the offer and the token sale took place on Binance at the end of 2019. This took place shortly after India lifted the ban on cryptocurrencies, which further escalated the growth of Matic network.

Matic is becoming the Layer 2 solution of choice for many projects building on Ethereum. All of this is taking place because of Matic's unique approach to the plasma scaling solution and the other useful products which the team has built for decentralised applications on Ethereum.

Plasma essentially involves creating a copy of the Ethereum blockchain called a 'child chain', this child chain periodically submits a snapshot of its state to its parent chain which is of course the Ethereum blockchain. If anything ever goes wrong in this plasma chain, the users are able to reference the most recent valid snapshot of the plasma chain on Ethereum, to restore operations and also reclaim their tokens. Joseph Poon has explained Plasma chain as the lower court of a judicial system, while on the other hand, the Ethereum blockchain acts as the Supreme court. Matic can use any cryptocurrency as its base layer.

Matic network's founders are genuinely passionate about the project and the future which they are building, and also about the decentralised user experience which they want to guarantee. The founders have predicted that it will take nearly a decade for the institutions really get comfortable with crypto.

OPINIONS OF THE GLOBAL PERSONALITIES ON BLOCKCHAIN AND CRYPTOCURRENCY

JACK MA (CO FOUNDER, ALIBABA GROUP)

"I think the blockchain is going to be a very critical technology for the future development of the world. It's not only about the financing, blockchain technology is not about Bitcoins, Bitcoin is just a small function of the blockchain technology. I am a strong believer of the blockchain technology".

DON TAPSCOTT (CEO, TAPSCOTT GROUP)

"This is not about Bitcoin or Crypto assets, it's the underlying blockchain technology, now people can trust each other and they can transact with anything, from money, to a music, from votes to their identities, peer to peer".

GARY VAYNERCHUK (ENTREPRENEUR & INTERNET PERSONALITY)

"Bitcoin is either myspace or its Facebook, I don't know. A blockchain is social media. So at the macro blockchain is going nowhere. Right, like blockchain's here to stay forever and it is a very big deal".

BEN GOERTZEL (AI RESEARCHER & CREATOR OF SOPHIA ROBOT)

"The business world of the future say 10 years from now is gonna run on smart contract, its gonna run on strong encryption and on Peer to Peer base consents mechanisms. So the core technologies underlying blockchain are going to provide everything just like the internet has just like the object oriented software has right now".

ROBERT KIYOSAKI (AMERICAN BUSINESSMAN & AUTHOR)

"So the choice, when I talk to people that what do you think will be here in 2040, which is 22 years from now, Will gold still be here? Well it's been here since eternity, Will the dollar be here? I don't think so, and Will the blockchain be here, I think so".

WINKLEVOSS TWINS (INTERNET ENTREPRENEURS)

"We think bitcoins as a digital gold 2.0, but it's money the first of the money that was every built purposely for internet. So it's sort of like what the email did to the standard mail. Cryptocurrency or Bitcoin does for money". "We still think that it's the bottom of the first inning, if you read this book you'll understand how we got here and how far it's come, but it's also sort of a beginning in a lot of ways".

BILL GATES (FOUNDER OF MICROSOFT)

"Well Bitcoins is exciting according to me because it shows how cheap it can be. A Bitcoin is better than currency and you don't have to be physically in the same place and of course for large transactions the currency can get pretty inconvenient, the customer we are talking about are trying to be anonymous, they are willing to be known so, the bitcoin technology is the key and you could add to it or you could build a similar technology, where there is enough attribution that people feel comfortable, this is nothing to do with terrorism or any type of money laundering".

RICHARD BRANSON (FOUNDER OF VIRGIN GROUP)

"Well I think it is working, and there will be other currencies like it that may, may be even better but in the meantime, there is a big industry around Bitcoin, people have made fortunes at Bitcoin, some people lost money out of Bitcoin, Yeah but it is quite Volatile, but people make money out of Volatility".

ELON MUSK (SPACEX AND TESLA)

"So where I see crypto is as respectively is a replacement for cash, but not as a replacement for as a primary, I do not see crypto as the primary database". "There are transactions which are not within the balance of the law and obviously there are many laws in different countries and normally cash is used for these transactions, but in order for the legal transactions to occur. You need an illegal to legal bridge". "I think it's going to be means to do illegal transactions, but that is not necessarily entirely bad, somethings shouldn't be illegal, ".

CHAMATH PALIHAPITIYA (VENTURE CAPITALIST)

"It's probably going to $100,000 then to $150,000 and then to $200,000, the time period I don't know, but it's going there and the reason is because every time you see stuff happening, it just reminds you that, WOW!, Our leaders are not that trustworthy as they used to be, and so just in case we really do need to have insurance which we can keep under the pillow which gives us access to an un corelated hedge, and its eventually going to transition to something really more important. But, now you just getting all the data points that prove this thing, it's just the fabric of society is afraid and until we figure out how to make it better, it's time to have just a little schmuck on the side, everybody is running in, it's just an incredible thing, I could have never imagined this".

MARK CUBAN (ENTREPRENEUR)

"If you're a true adventurer, you might take 10% and put it in Bitcoin or Ethereum, but if you do that you gotta pretend that you've lost your money and it's like collecting art, collecting baseball cards, it's like collecting shoes, something is worth when somebody is willing to pay the money, it's a flyer but I would limit it to 10%".

PETER THIEL (FOUNDERS FUND PARTNER)

"I am sceptical of most of the crypto currencies, I think that people are a little bit maybe under estimating bitcoin, because it is like a reserve form of money, it is like gold, and it's just a store of value, and there are about $70 Billion worth of Bitcoin in the world and there is $9 trillion worth of Gold, and if Bitcoin ends up being the cyber equivalent of gold, it has a great potential left, it may be very underestimated. It can never be deluded by the government, it can never be hacked and it's a form of money and is secure in an absolute way ".

WARREN BUFFET (BERKSHIRE HATHAWAY)

"It is not a currency, it is not made for the test pf currency, I would not be surprised if it is not around in 10 or 20 years, people say I'll sell you good in exchange of Bitcoins, but they change the price of those every time the price of dollar changes, they're pricing it off the dollar, they can say I'll sell it to you of barrels of oil, but every time the price of oil changes the number of barrel changes, the oil is not the currency, it is all a bubble which will not end well". "When you buy a farm, you look at the crop every year, and what prices are and you decide whether it was satisfactory, you look to the asset itself, and what it produces for you, when we buy a business, we look at what the business earns and how we feel about it in terms of what we pay, but if we buy something which we do not have at the end of the period we not only have what we bought for the first place, but we have something which the asset produced, the crypto asset itself is creating nothing".

Cryptocurrencies have clearly brought a financial revolution in the society, the most innovative technology which came with the introduction of Bitcoin, was the Blockchain System. I am a huge admirer and a strong supporter of the Blockchain Technology and I believe that it could further revolutionise every sector of the society.

The value of money is decreasing year by year, because of the continuous influx of cash in the market, produced by the government. Since, the cash is unlimited and can be produced without any limitation, it will always decrease the value of money over the period of time because it is so abundant. On the other hand Bitcoin which is considered to be the 'digital gold' is limited in number and supply, that is why its value will keep increasing with its demand and time. There are some other valuable cryptocurrencies as well which are limited in number, these act as a token of value, which the people have agreed to collectively and are willing to have transactions using the same.

The decentralised method is truly revolutionary as nobody can regulate or control it, so there can be no corruption at all, the blockchain technology is the icing on the cake, because it is almost impossible to hack into the blocks and change the entire chain at the same time.

This Digital token of value is of great innovation as you don't need any place to physically store it, hide it, keep a check on, and is only accessible to you. The blessing in disguise is the volatility which can earn you sweet profits in the short run, but that should not be a main stream approach, and should just be a by-product of investing in the crypto market.

The focus of the investor should be on the cryptos which actually provide 'real value' and will impact or benefit the society's future at large. There are a majority of crypto which are baseless and provide no intrinsic value, and fake hypes are being created just to cash some money out, which I think causes harm to the market sentiments. People with influence should not indulge in paid promotions of the crypto which they have no idea about, because they influence the market a lot, the approach should be of value investing because only value can create value.

Influential people who are using their face value on social media to pump these cryptocurrencies does not help in promoting the core value, for which it were made in the first place. This is wrongly influencing the mentality of the society, as majority of them are 'gambling' and not 'investing' in the innovative and revolutionary technology which will provide so much value for the generations to come. Due to this negative approach, the decentralised mediums are used for doing illegal activities, because of which the government of many countries are against the use of crypto currency in general. Banning the use of crypto currency would decelerate the technological advancements in our society and we would not be able to use this genius of an innovation for the betterment of our future.

Some people including many great personalities, like Warren Buffet, even think that it is just a bubble and it will not end well as the collapse will lead to a lot of financial loss to the people who have invested heavily in it. Many speculations have also been made, that this might be the biggest scam on the face of mankind, of which everybody is a part and promoter. To outrightly ban the use of crypto would be a wrong decision for the non-supporting countries, they could levy taxes on them and help in their own economic growth. There should be a proper committee which takes the advice from people and make certain regulations on the use of crypto, and proper laws should be made on it. Experiments with the technology should be made in order to extract the best of the crypto currency market, rather than banning it or completely supporting it.

At last, I would say, that whatever investments one makes in this market, should be value based and purely on the research which the individual does and believes in, hearsay will only increase the volatility even more, which will further tarnish the image of Crypto market and portray it as a platform to gamble. People who invest their money without research would eventually lose their money and time, sooner or later. The message which I want to convey with this book, is that there is no harm in experimenting with new things, but without proper research and calculative risk, people will make a fool out of themselves, so I would request you all to research and then think whether to invest in the cryptocurrency or not.

www.ingramcontent.com/pod-product-compliance
Lightning Source LLC
Chambersburg PA
CBHW020707180526
45163CB00008B/2976